I can count

Ray Gibson

Designed and illustrated by Amanda Barlow
Edited by Jenny Tyler

Contents

I can count

You can follow the instructions in this book to print fun pictures, each based on a different number. Most of the printing is done with potatoes cut in half and your fingers. You will need a paintbrush to finish off some of the pictures.

Perhaps you can think of other things to print or paint for each number too.

Opposite you can see some tips on potato printing. You will need a big potato and a small one. Ask an adult to cut them for you. You can keep your potatoes in the refrigerator for a few days. Wash, dry and wrap them up first.

If you don't want to get your paints out, you can use the pictures in this book for counting practice.

Potato printing

1. Lay some kitchen paper towels onto a thick pile of newspaper.

2. Pour paint on top. Spread out with the back of a spoon.

3. Cut a potato in half. If you like you can make a handle by cutting it like this.

4. Lay your printing paper onto another pile of newspaper.

5. Press the potato in the paint. Then press it onto the printing paper.

6. You can print two or three times before putting more paint on.

I can count to 1

1. Print a body with a big potato.

2. Add a tail with a brush.

3. Finger paint a white eye.

4. When dry, add a black middle to the eye.

5. Paint a big mouth with a brush.

6. Finger paint a waterspout.

1 whale

I can count to 2

1. Print a black body with a big potato. Leave to dry.

2. Print a white tummy with a smaller potato.

3. Add a yellow beak with a brush.

4. Paint 2 black flippers.

5. Paint 2 orange feet.

6. Paint a white and black eye.

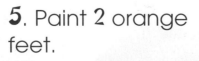

2 penguins

I can count to 3

1. Print a body with a big potato.

2. Print a head with a small potato.

3. Paint a beak and an eye.

4. Paint 3 head feathers and 3 tail feathers.

5. Paint some legs with a brush.

6. Add 3 toes to each leg.

3 birds

I can count to 4

1. Print a body. Print eyes on top with your finger.

2. Paint 4 legs with a brush.

3. Paint some toes on each leg.

4. Print white spots in the eyes with your finger.

5. Print black dots in the eyes. Paint a mouth with a brush.

6. Use your finger to print 4 spots on the tummy.

4 frogs

I can count to 5

Flowers

1. Print a flower middle with your finger.

2. Print **5** petals with a small potato.

3. Paint a stalk with a brush.

Bees

1. Print **5** bee bodies with your finger.

2. Finger paint wings on the bees.

3. Paint black stripes with a brush.

5 flowers

I can count to 6

1. Print a cat's face with a potato. Add ears with a finger or brush.

2. Print white eyes with dark dots. Use your finger.

3. Paint a black nose with a brush.

4. Add a mouth, and 6 whiskers.

Mice

1. Print 6 mice with your finger.

2. Finger paint an ear. Add tail, nose and eye.

6 cats

I can count to 7

1. Print a body with a big potato.

2. Print an eye with your finger.

3. Paint a tail and a fin with a brush.

4. Paint a mouth with a brush.

5. Paint **7** spines with a brush.

6. Print **7** spots with your finger.

7 fish

I can count to 8

1. Use a big potato to print a body.

2. Paint 2 stalks. Print eyes on top.

3. Print the middles with your finger.

4. Paint the mouth.

5. Paint 8 legs.

6. Put claws on the top legs.

8 crabs

I can count to 9

1. Print a small potato 3 times for a body.

2. Print a head. Finger paint a pointed tail.

3. Print eyes with your finger.

4. Print dots in the eyes. Paint a nose and a mouth.

5. Paint 9 legs. Put 3 on each part of the body.

6. Print 9 feet with your finger.

9 caterpillars

I can count to 10

1. Print a head with your fingertip.

2. Paint a body with your finger.

3. Print wings with a potato.

4. Paint 2 feelers with a brush.

5. Print 10 big spots with your finger - **5** on each wing.

6. Paint 10 dots inside the spots.

10 butterflies

I can count to 20

There are 20 ducks on these two pages. Can you count them all?

Now count how many ducks are swimming.

How many ducks have a yellow beak?

How many ducks have yellow feet?

How many ducks are pecking corn?

How many ducks have a worm?

See page 32 for how to paint ducks like these.

I can count to 30

There are 30 fish on these two pages. Can you count them?

Now count how many of them have a green tail.

Find out how to print fish on page 32

How many fish are swimming from left to right?
How many yellow fish are there?
How many fish have a yellow tail?

I can count to 40

There are 40 mice on these two pages. Can you count them?

Now count how many mice have a white tail.
How many pink mice are there?

Look back at page 14 to find out how to print mice.

How many mice have purple ears?
How many mice have pink ears?
How many mice have white ears?
How many mice have a piece of cheese?

I can count to 50

There are **50** spiders on these two pages. Can you count them all?

Now count how many black spiders there are.
How many spiders have pink legs?

Find out how to print spiders on page 32

How many spiders have green eyes?
How many spiders have black legs?
How many spiders are green with yellow legs?
How many yellow spiders are there?

Duck, fish and spider

For a duck

1. Print a body with a quarter of a potato.

2. Use a small potato to print a head.

3. Paint a beak and 2 feet.

4. Add an eye with your finger.

For a fish

1. Print a body with a potato.

2. Print a tail with a quarter of a potato. Paint an eye.

For a spider

1. Print a body with a potato.

2. Paint 8 legs and 2 eyes.